Emerge BRIGHTER

Reveal Your Potential
Through Strategic Life Planning

Shannon Laine Smock

The vision of Emerge Brighter is to create a global network of empowered women who are shaping a brighter future for themselves and others.

Emerge BRIGHTER

Reveal Your Potential Through Strategic Life Planning

Shannon Laine Smock

Copyright © 2024 Emerge Brighter, LLC
St. Louis, Missouri
emergebrighter.com

All rights reserved. No part of this publication may be reproduced, stored in a retrieval system, or transmitted, in any form or by any means, electronic, mechanical, photocopying, recording, or otherwise, without the prior written permission of Emerge Brighter, LLC.

ISBN: 978-1-7330837-2-0
PRINTED IN USA

CONTENTS

MODULE INTRODUCTION 5
    1. Strategic Life Planning 6
    2. Mindset Quiz 7
    3. Old Way vs. New Way 8

MODULE 1 9
    1. Self Reflection 11
    2. Four Key Pillars
        • Purpose 14
        • Vision 18
        • Values 23
        • Mission 26

MODULE 2 28
    1. SWOT 30
    2. Strategic Areas of Focus 36
    3. SMART KPIs 39
    4. My Action Plan 44

MODULE 3 48
    1. One-Page Strategic Life Plan 50
    2. Strategic Dashboard 52
    3. Notes 55

Hello!

I founded Emerge Brighter in 2019 after my best friend Katrina and I took a girls' trip to Aruba. What we thought was going to be just a simple, relaxing getaway turned into a life-changing Aha! moment. When I arrived in Aruba I was exhausted, overworked, and feeling like I was failing as a mom. I'd already failed at my marriage, and my career was just not fulfilling me anymore. You would never have known it on the outside, and I kept myself so busy that I never had the time to process everything I was feeling.

In just a couple of days, Katrina and I led ourselves through reflecting on where we had been, established our vision and goals for the next year, and identified that our individual health and well-being must come before all else. By the end of 2019, I had achieved every single one of the goals I set in Aruba, including improving my health, getting my son into a new school system for him to thrive, publishing my first book, and starting my own company.

Moreover, in 2020, I was honored as one of *St. Louis Business Journal's* 40 Under 40 and also found the love of my life. I just wanted to bottle the keys to all of this success up so I could share it with others. So, I did and this is for you.

Shannon Laine Smock

emergebrighter.com
shannon@emergebrighter.com

MODULE

INTRODUCTION

Strategic Life Planning

One of the most important steps in developing a strategic life plan is understanding that this will be a continuous process. Once you develop your plan you will want to ensure that you can regularly review your progress. This will take time, effort, and a commitment that you will be honest with yourself throughout this journey.

Strategic life planning clarifies who you are, what you want to achieve, and how you will do it; it also helps you to understand what success will look like.

Emerge Brighter's strategic life planning process consists of the following:

- Self-Reflection
- 4 Key Pillars
- SWOT Analysis
- Strategic Areas of Focus
- Key Performance Indicators
- Action Plan
- Strategic One-Pager
- Dashboard

Are you ready to get started?

Your Thoughts:

Mindset Quiz

How do you typically approach goal setting?

- I set ambitious goals but struggle to create a clear road map to achieve them.
- I prefer to go with the flow and see where life takes me.
- I break down large goals into smaller, more manageable steps with timelines.
- I set goals but often get discouraged by setbacks.

When faced with challenges, what is your initial reaction?

- I analyze the situation and brainstorm solutions.
- I feel overwhelmed and avoid making decisions.
- I seek advice and support from trusted individuals.
- I give up easily and move on to something else.

How comfortable are you with reflecting on your progress and adjusting your plans?

- I regularly evaluate my progress and adapt my approach as needed.
- I find it difficult to revisit past decisions and correct my course.
- I prefer to stick to the plan I initially create, regardless of new information.
- I rarely reflect on my progress and may miss opportunities for improvement.

How do you view your long-term vision for the future?

- I have a clear vision for my future and am actively working toward it.
- I have a vague idea of what I want but haven't developed a concrete plan.
- I believe the future is unpredictable and focus on the present moment.
- I feel uncertain about my long-term goals and direction.

Strategic Life Planning
Old Way vs. New Way

THEN

Focus on rigid, long-term goals, which are set in stone

Utilize linear planning with detailed steps

Focus on past failures and shortcomings, leading to discouragement and negativity

Acknowledge that procrastination and perfectionism can stall progress due to fear of starting or making mistakes

Overemphasize traditional milestones like career paths or material possessions

VS.

NOW

Encourage SMART goals allowing for adjustments based on progress and evolving priorities

Utilize mind maps and vision boards for a more visual and interactive planning experience

Emphasize growth mindset, analyzing past experiences for lessons learned and celebrating successes

Embrace small, consistent steps and celebrate incremental progress

Integrate personal values, passions, and purpose into goal setting alongside practical considerations like finances and career

MODULE 1

Self-reflection is like a flower turning toward the sun; it's in those moments of introspection that we find the light needed for growth and blossoming.

Emerge Brighter

Self-Reflection

Self-reflection provides clarity, direction, and purpose. By taking the time to reflect on your past experiences, accomplishments, and challenges, you can identify patterns, preferences, and areas of interest. This self-awareness enables you to make informed decisions about your goals, your aspirations, and the steps needed to achieve them. Self-reflection also allows you to align your future plans with your values, passions, and strengths, leading to greater fulfillment and success in your endeavors. Let's start with a self-reflection activity. This activity allows you to reflect on your personal growth over the past year and can be done solo or with the help of a partner. Feel free to use the note space on the next page to work through this activity.

ROSE
What was something positive or rewarding about the past year?

THORN
What were the challenges or difficulties you faced?

BUD
What did you learn or how did you grow from these experiences?

If you are working with a partner, complete the following steps:

Partner Sharing: Take turns sharing responses with your partner. Listen actively and avoid interrupting.

Open Discussion: After sharing, discuss your experiences with each other. Consider these prompts:

- Did anything surprise you about your partner's experience?
- Can you offer any insights to each other?
- How can you support each other's growth moving forward?

REFLECTION NOTES

> True happiness is found in the pursuit of your purpose, where every moment becomes a testament to living a life of meaning and passion.
>
> Emerge Brighter

KEY PILLAR 1

Find Your Purpose

Let's focus on identifying your purpose. I do not want you to think about what you do for a job. Your purpose is your WHY. It is the reason you get up every single day. It drives everything you do and it should be inspirational.

Purpose

The next page includes ten questions for you to answer. Try to come up with several answers to each question. The questions may seem redundant, but please do your best to keep searching for answers. By asking "Why?" multiple times and delving deeper with each question, you can uncover underlying motivations, interests, and values.

Trust Yourself

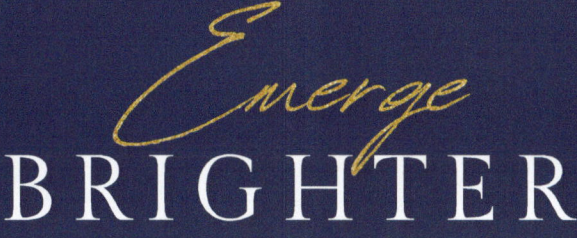

Purpose Questions

1. When do I feel like my happiest self?

2. What activities bring me the most joy?

3. In what ways do I make a difference?

4. Why am I here?

5. Why does my impact matter?

6. What keeps me motivated?

7. What issues in the world ignite a passion or drive within me?

8. What legacy do I want to leave behind?

9. What makes me uniquely me, and how can I use that uniqueness to serve a greater purpose?

10. When have I truly felt alive? Share a story.

Crafting a Purpose Statement

Look at the responses to the questions you just answered. What themes stand out? What resonates with you? Work on creating a short, clear, inspirational purpose statement from your answers. If you're not a wordsmith, do not underestimate the potential of using an AI generator to help you find the right wording.

Use the lines provided to craft your purpose statement:

Craft a vision that reflects your strength and potential. When you see yourself through the lens of empowerment, you unlock the boundless possibilities within you.

Emerge Brighter

KEY PILLAR 2

Visualize Your Vision

Your vision is the future that you want to achieve. It is what you want to be. It should be forward-looking and inspirational as well as ambitious and big but not too big for you to achieve it. It serves as your North Star.

Vision

Vision statements are simple, short, and clear. Your vision should align with your goals and should project five to ten years into the future. On the next page you will find a vision board to help you outline some of the things most important to you.

Paint It Clearly

Vision Board

Travel

GOALS

FAMILY

Hobbies

CAREER

RELATIONSHIPS

HEALTH

Money

Do more of what you love.

Crafting Your Personal Vision Statement with Rose-Colored Glasses

Part 1: Set your time machine to ten years in the future. When you open the doors to the time machine, you step out into your ideal future. What does your life look like? What have you achieved? What impact have you had? Use the space below to write freely about your visualization.

_____
_____
_____
_____
_____
_____
_____
_____
_____

Part 2: Review your freewriting and highlight or underline key phrases, themes, or words that stand out to you. Consider categorizing these key elements (for example, personal achievements, relationships, emotions, values).

_____
_____
_____
_____
_____
_____
_____
_____

Crafting a Vision Statement

Look at yourself and your writing through rose-colored glasses. Think about how you would frame your vision positively and optimistically. Write a draft of your personal vision statement, focusing on positivity and empowerment.

Use the lines provided to craft your vision statement:

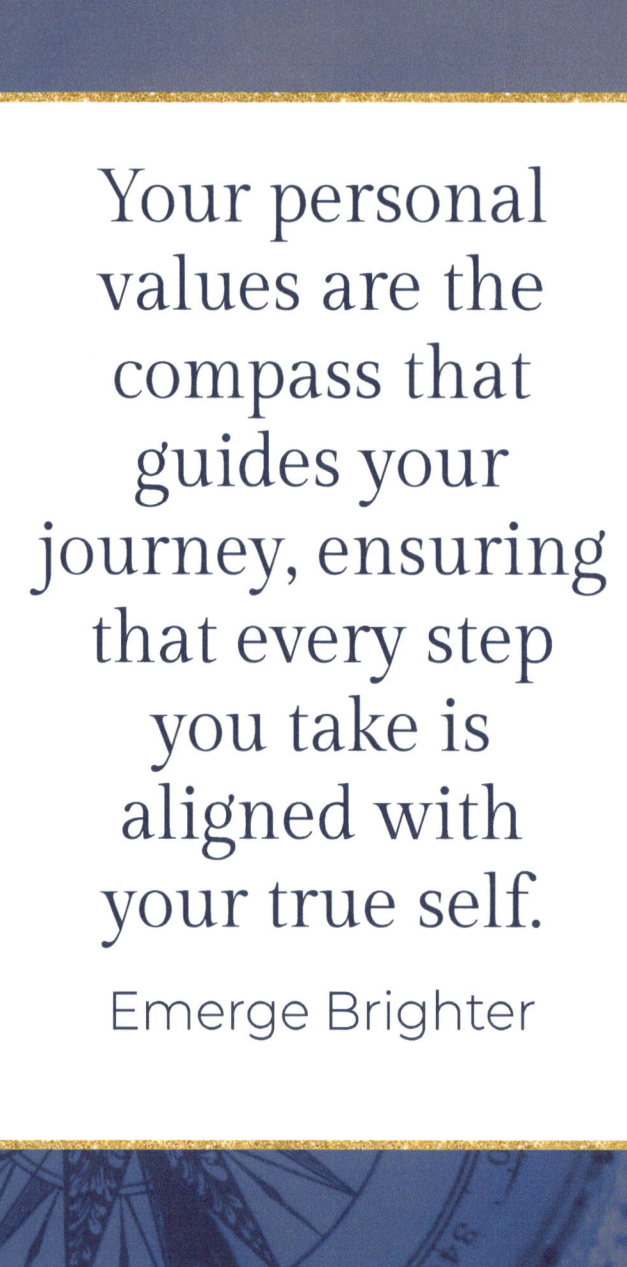

> Your personal values are the compass that guides your journey, ensuring that every step you take is aligned with your true self.
>
> Emerge Brighter

KEY PILLAR 3

Values to Live By

Values are what you believe and how you behave. They should be unique to you. Your values should be so important to you that you would be willing to walk away from the people, jobs, or things in your life that ask you to go against your values.

Values

Patrick Lencioni, an American author who specializes in business management, has a great article on company values titled "Make Your Values Mean Something." He refers to Permission to Play values; these are values you should possess just by being a decent human being. This concept absolutely translates to personal values. Rather than listing honesty, kindness, and respect as your values—these values are simply part of being a decent person—consider this: what values set you apart from everyone else?

Uniquely You

Value Creator

Fill in the blank with a value so important to you that you would walk away from people, jobs, or places that don't align with it. Try to come up with four personal values that resonate deeply with you.

Example, "If it doesn't **support my growth**, I am out."

If it doesn't _____, I'm out.

Value 1

Value 2

Value 3

Value 4

Reflection:
- Why did you choose this value?

- How has this value influenced your past decisions?

- How will this value guide your future actions?

> The difference between goals and mission is reflected in the difference between I want to get married and I want to have a successful marriage.
>
> Author Unknown

KEY PILLAR 4

Mission

The fourth and final key pillar is creating your mission statement. Your mission statement should answer who you are, what you do, and what impact you will have. It should be short but broad and not too limiting. When someone hears your mission statement, you want that person to have a clear and inspiring image of you. Let's dive into what makes up a great mission statement with the Mission ABCs.

Mission ABCs

A. Activity
The Activity broadly states what you do to achieve your vision. Think about the core actions you take to fulfill your mission. **Do you educate, inspire, prepare, guide, empower, or something else? What is it that you do?**

B. Beneficiary
The Beneficiary is the who or what you do your activity for. **Is it for yourself, your family, women, professionals, children, or others? Identify the primary recipient(s) or stakeholder(s) of your efforts. Who benefits from what you do?**

C. Change
The Change refers to the impact you want to have on the beneficiary. **What difference do you want to make? What positive transformation are you striving to achieve: empowerment, personal growth, professional success, or something else?**

Purpose-Driven Impact

Craft Your Mission Statement

Step 1: Define Your Activity
Write down what you do to achieve your vision:

Step 2: Identify Your Beneficiary
Who benefits from your work?

Step 3: Determine the Change You Want to Create
What impact do you want to have on your beneficiary?

Use your answers from the steps above to craft your mission statement:

"My mission is to [Activity] for [Beneficiary] in order to [Change]."

My mission is to _____ for _____ in order to _____.

Feel free to use the lines below to craft alternate variations.

_____

_____

_____

_____

_____

_____

_____

MODULE 2

Just as a butterfly emerges stronger and more beautiful from its cocoon, embracing your strengths and weaknesses will transform you into your most vibrant self.

Emerge Brighter

Harnessing Self-Awareness

In order to have a strategic life plan that is aligned and set up for success, you should conduct a SWOT—Strengths, Weaknesses, Opportunities, Threats—analysis. Doing a SWOT analysis allows you to dive deep into the internal and external factors that have the ability to impact your vision and goals.

SWOT

A SWOT analysis helps you understand your internal strengths and weaknesses, as well as external opportunities and threats. Knowing yourself is the first step to achieving your goals. As you work through each section you can use this awareness to create a strategic life plan and make meaningful progress in your life.

Unlocking Potential

Emerge BRIGHTER

SWOT Questions

1. Reflect on your Strengths:
- What are you really good at?
- If you asked a trusted friend, what would that person say your strengths are?
- Are you creative, good at problem-solving, or a great communicator?
- Do you have a great sense of humor?
- What resources do you have?

Write down at least four strengths:
-
-
-
-

2. Reflect on your Weaknesses:
- Where do I need to improve?
- What resources am I lacking?
- Do I lack self-confidence?
- Am I impulsive or disorganized?
- Do I procrastinate, overthink things, or struggle with time management?

Write down at least four weaknesses:
-
-
-
-

SWOT Questions *continued*

3. **Reflect on Opportunities:**

- What opportunities are available to you right now?
- Are there any upcoming events, courses, or networking opportunities that can help you grow?
- Are there any gaps in the market you can fill with your skills?

Write down at least four opportunities:

-
-
-
-

4. **Reflect on Threats:**

- What challenges are you currently facing?
- Are there any obstacles that could hinder your progress?
- Are there external factors like economic conditions or competition that could impact you?

Write down at least four threats:

-
-
-
-

5. Analysis and Reflection

- Review your lists and reflect on how your strengths can help you overcome weaknesses, capitalize on opportunities, and mitigate threats.
- Consider how you can turn weaknesses into strengths and threats into opportunities.

Creating Alignment

Before you move on to the next activity, review your four key pillars side by side with your SWOT analysis. Use the lines below to summarize what you have accomplished so far.

Purpose:

Vision:

Values:

1.   2.   3.   4.

Mission:

Strengths	Weaknesses	Opportunities	Threats

Clarity and Focus

Review

When reviewing everything you have created so far—your purpose, vision, values, mission, and SWOT analysis—consider the following key points to ensure alignment:

Consistency:
Do your vision and mission statements reflect your core values?

Clarity:
Are your purpose, vision, and mission statements clear and concise?

Cohesion:
Is there a clear and logical flow from your purpose to your vision, mission, and SWOT analysis?

Inspiration:
Do your vision and mission inspire and motivate you?

Are they compelling enough to drive you toward your goals?

Impact:
Is the intended impact of your mission clear and measurable?

Take the time you need to ensure everything you have developed up to this point is in alignment and that you are ready to move forward. If anything needs to be tweaked, now is the time to adjust.

Like a magnifying glass that concentrates sunlight into a powerful beam, your strategic areas of focus concentrate your energy toward your vision.

Choose them wisely and illuminate your path to success.

Emerge Brighter

Strategic Areas of Focus

After developing your four key pillars and completing a SWOT analysis, the next part of the *Emerge Brighter Strategic Life Planning* process is to explicitly state your strategic areas of focus. These serve as the framework for your plan and include high-priority areas you need to focus on right now to move you closer to achieving your vision.

Illuminate Your Path

What four areas in your life do you need to focus on right now to ultimately achieve your future vision? Some areas to consider might be your family, finances, professional development, career, or health. Once you have identified your four strategic areas of focus, take a moment to reflect on why each area is important and how focusing on it will contribute to achieving your overall vision. Your strategic areas of focus are going to guide the future decisions you make.

Be Intentional

Strategic Areas of Focus Questions

- Brainstorm potential strategic areas of focus based on the key aspects of your vision and the opportunities and challenges highlighted in your SWOT analysis.

- Narrow down your focus to four priority areas that you believe are critical for moving closer to your vision.

- Write down each strategic area of focus in the designated spaces below.

- Keep these strategic areas of focus in mind as you develop your strategic life plan and be sure to make decisions that align with your vision.

Strategic Areas of Focus:
1.
2.
3.
4.

Reflection Questions:

- Why is each strategic area of focus important for achieving your future vision?

- How do you envision focusing on these areas will impact your journey toward your goals?

- What actions can you take to prioritize and address each strategic area of focus in your daily life?

- How will you measure progress and success in each area to ensure alignment with your overall vision?

Identifying your strategic areas of focus is crucial to aligning your efforts with your vision and ensuring that your actions are purposeful and directed toward achieving your long-term goals.

> By setting SMART goals, we harness the power of intention and strategy, transforming visions into tangible realities.
>
> Emerge Brighter

SMART KPIs

Key Performance Indicators or KPIs are measurable performance outcomes. You must be able to measure a KPI to determine if you are achieving success. If it can't be measured, it is not a KPI.

SMART is an acronym for **Specific, Measurable, Achievable, Relevant,** and **Time Based.** Your KPIs are how you are going to evaluate the success of your strategic life plan, so they must be SMART.

Make It Measurable

The object of this next activity is to identify four SMART Key Performance Indicators (KPIs) for each of your four strategic areas of focus. When you are finished, you will have sixteen KPIs.

Measurable Milestones

Review Your Strategic Areas of Focus:

Begin by listing your four strategic areas of focus in the boxes on the next page.

Brainstorm Potential KPIs:
For each Strategic Area of Focus, brainstorm potential KPIs that could indicate progress and success. Consider what success looks like for each area.

Set Four SMART KPIs for Each Focus Area:
Select the four most relevant and impactful KPIs for each strategic area.

Ensure each KPI you set adheres to the SMART criteria:

- **Specific:** Clearly defines what you want to achieve
  Detail the goal

- **Measurable:** Includes criteria to measure progress
  Define the metrics

- **Achievable:** Realistic and attainable
  Explain why it's realistic

- **Relevant:** Aligns with your vision and strategic areas of focus
  Align with vision

- **Time-Based:** Has a clear deadline or time frame
  Set the deadline

Review and Adjust:
Review your KPIs to ensure they are aligned with your overall vision and strategic life plan.

Adjust any KPIs that do not fully meet the SMART criteria.

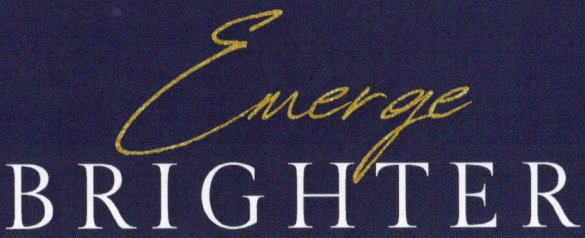

SMART KPIs

SPECIFIC	MEASURABLE	ACHIEVABLE	RELEVANT	TIME-BASED
Is your KPI specific? Does it state exactly what you want to achieve?	Can you quantify the progress of your KPI? Can you measure it?	Is your KPI "right-sized"? Meaning, can you successfully achieve it?	Is your KPI relevant to the Strategic Area of Focus you have identified?	Can you successfully achieve your KPI in a specified amount of time?

FOCUS AREA 1:

FOCUS AREA 2:

FOCUS AREA 3:

FOCUS AREA 4:

KPI Ideas: List potential KPIs here

1.
2.
3.
4.
5.

KPI Ideas: List potential KPIs here

1.
2.
3.
4.
5.

KPI Ideas: List potential KPIs here

1.
2.
3.
4.
5.

KPI Ideas: List potential KPIs here

1.
2.
3.
4.
5.

SMART KPIs *continued*

Select four SMART KPIs for each focus area:

Focus Area 1:

- KPI 1:
- KPI 2:
- KPI 3:
- KPI 4:

Focus Area 2:

- KPI 1:
- KPI 2:
- KPI 3:
- KPI 4:

Focus Area 3:

- KPI 1:
- KPI 2:
- KPI 3:
- KPI 4:

Focus Area 4:

- KPI 1:
- KPI 2:
- KPI 3:
- KPI 4:

Review and Adjust:
Double-check each KPI to ensure it meets the SMART criteria.
Make necessary adjustments for clarity and alignment with your vision.

PRIORITIZE NEXT STEPS

You have worked hard to develop the main components of your strategic life plan, but you are not finished yet.

Next, you will need to determine and prioritize the actions that must be completed to achieve the goals you have already defined.

You are now going to focus on developing your Action Plan. For this activity, think about what activities you will need to accomplish to successfully achieve each KPI. Be as creative as you want.

You can create a step-by-step list that includes a timeline or draw out a mind map of how you will accomplish each goal. Feel free to use extra paper if you need more room.

When you have completed an action plan for each KPI, you will move on to the final phase of Emerge Brighter's Strategic Life Planning process by pulling it all together in a Strategic One-Pager and developing your Strategic Dashboard.

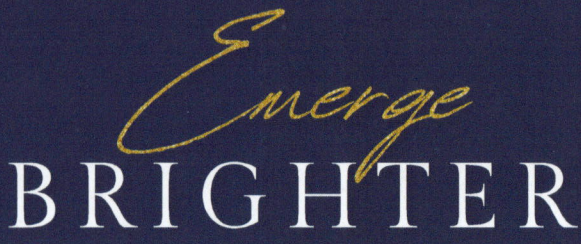

My Action Plan

STRATEGIC AREA OF FOCUS 1

KPI 1:

KPI 2:

KPI 3:

KPI 4:

MY ACTION PLAN

What activities will you need to accomplish to successfully complete your KPIs? Be as specific as possible. Include a timeline and identify if other individuals will be responsible for helping you complete each step.

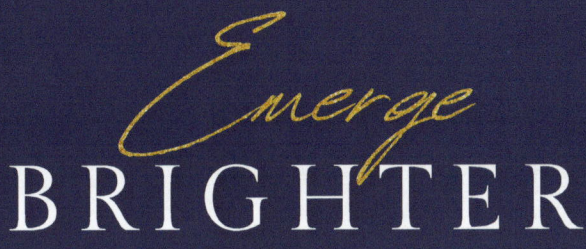

My Action Plan

STRATEGIC AREA OF FOCUS 2

KPI 1:

KPI 2:

KPI 3:

KPI 4:

MY ACTION PLAN

What activities will you need to accomplish to successfully complete your KPIs? Be as specific as possible. Include a timeline and identify if other individuals will be responsible for helping you complete each step.

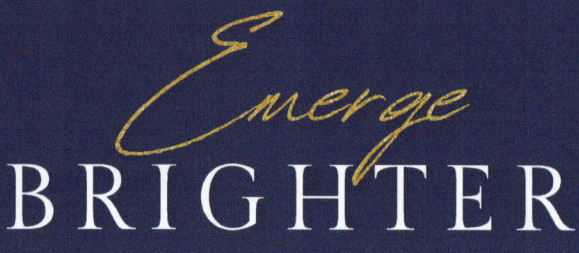

My Action Plan

STRATEGIC AREA OF FOCUS 3

KPI 1:

KPI 2:

KPI 3:

KPI 4:

MY ACTION PLAN

What activities will you need to accomplish to successfully complete your KPIs? Be as specific as possible. Include a timeline and identify if other individuals will be responsible for helping you complete each step.

My Action Plan

STRATEGIC AREA OF FOCUS 4

KPI 1:

KPI 2:

KPI 3:

KPI 4:

MY ACTION PLAN

What activities will you need to accomplish to successfully complete your KPIs? Be as specific as possible. Include a timeline and identify if other individuals will be responsible for helping you complete each step.

MODULE 3

Pulling It All Together

You have successfully developed your four Key Pillars, completed a SWOT analysis, identified your Strategic Areas of Focus, developed SMART Key Performance Indicators (KPIs) to measure your success, and created an Action Plan to achieve each KPI. Now it is time to pull it all together. You will now take all of your completed worksheets and summarize your final product into Emerge Brighter's Strategic One-Pager. This is the document you need to put in a place where you can see it every single day.

Well Done!

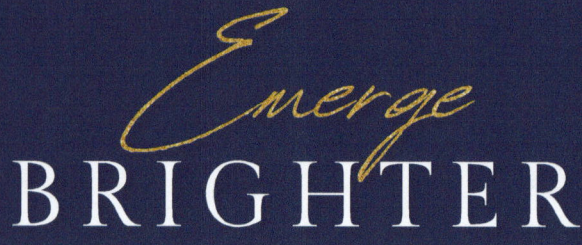

One-Page Strategic Life Plan

Purpose:

Vision:

| VALUE 1: | VALUE 2: | VALUE 3: | VALUE 4: |

Mission:

| FOCUS #1 | FOCUS #2 | FOCUS #3 | FOCUS #4 |

| FOCUS #1 KPIs | FOCUS #2 KPIs | FOCUS #3 KPIs | FOCUS #4 KPIs |

| ACTION PLAN | ACTION PLAN | ACTION PLAN | ACTION PLAN |

Track Your Progress

The last component of the *Emerge Brighter Strategic Life Planning* process is to develop a dashboard to evaluate and review your progress for all of your strategic areas of focus and the KPI's that you identified for each.

Establish a Baseline

For each KPI, you will develop a baseline. It may be as simple as writing down a number identifying where you are now, such as your current 5K running time. You may have to develop one from scratch or make your own projection. What is important is that you are consistent in how you track the numbers moving forward.

Pull It All Together

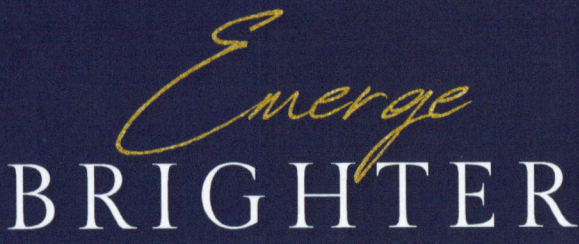

Strategic Dashboard

Strategic Areas of Focus	Key Performance Indicators [KPIs]	Baseline Year _____	[Year to Date]	Year ___	Year ___	Year ___
Focus #1	KPI 1					
	KPI 2					
	KPI 3					
	KPI 4					

Strategic Areas of Focus	Key Performance Indicators [KPIs]	Baseline Year _____	[Year to Date]	Year ___	Year ___	Year ___
Focus #2	KPI 1					
	KPI 2					
	KPI 3					
	KPI 4					

Strategic Areas of Focus	Key Performance Indicators [KPIs]	Baseline Year _____	[Year to Date]	Year ___	Year ___	Year ___
Focus #3	KPI 1					
	KPI 2					
	KPI 3					
	KPI 4					

Strategic Areas of Focus	Key Performance Indicators [KPIs]	Baseline Year _____	[Year to Date]	Year ___	Year ___	Year ___
Focus #4	KPI 1					
	KPI 2					
	KPI 3					
	KPI 4					

Celebrate Your Success

Congratulations!

You have completed your strategic life plan. Please remember, the strategic life planning process is never completely finished. Ensure that you have a process to continuously review your progress and adjust when needed. Consider adding the tasks from your action plan to your calendar or create a task checklist to help you stay on track, and don't forget to put your one-page strategic life plan somewhere you can see it every day.

For best results, you'll want to complete the *Emerge Brighter Strategic Life Planning* process each year, but you are free to design yours as a multiyear plan. Just remember to stay flexible, regularly revisit your goals, and adjust your focus as needed to stay aligned with your evolving vision and priorities.

Thank you!

Thank you for choosing Emerge Brighter to guide you through the Strategic Life Planning process. We hope that by identifying your strengths, weaknesses, strategic areas of focus, and setting SMART KPIs, you feel empowered and equipped to achieve your vision. Remember, this journey is about revealing your potential, spreading joy, and making a meaningful impact in your life and the lives of others. We are honored to be part of your path to personal and professional success. Let's continue to Emerge Brighter together!

Contact:
EMERGEBRIGHTER.COM
SHANNON@EMERGEBRIGHTER.COM

NOTES

NOTES

NOTES

NOTES

www.ingramcontent.com/pod-product-compliance
Lightning Source LLC
Chambersburg PA
CBHW041957150426
43193CB00003B/48